AKRASIA

RUTH KHAWLHRING

Made with ♥ on the Notion Press Platform
www.notionpress.com

To Taurus,

The iron string of my heart vibrates to the fiber of your entire being

Foreword

Also by the author

The Trouble Maker

Shallow

Ignoria

Jengkha Diary

Part One

if i possess all the time in the world to write about you, they would still not be enough, if i possess the ability to speak every language known to man, they still would not be enough, and even if i have all the riches and splendor the flesh could want, they still would mean nothing if i did not have you. you bring meaning to my life, the simplest song could mean more to me than the world if it is a song associated with you, all the great writings in the world would be for nought since they were not written for you, all the stars in the sky only matter if they shine for you, the moon would have little significance unless it serves as a light to guide your way home at night, the trees have small avail if not they provide a shadow to protect you from the sun's exposure, music's artistry vamooses if they do not make your heart dance, and the world only has meaning because you reside in it.

you paint my soul with cosmos dust
there are not enough words
in the human language
that i can string together
to explain how scintillatingly
you colored my heart of black and white

loving you is embedded in my soul
like a drapery woven right into the core of my heart
i do not know how to stop it

even if i were to live a thousand years
and a thousand lives
i would still know you in every lifetime
and i would still want you in each of them

look at the sky full of stars
at the oceans blanketing the shores
at the lofty cordillera of mountains
how majestic God's creations are
and yet
just like that, you have become the most beautiful
of God's creations i have ever known

a fire that cannot be extinguished
a flower that is blooming through all seasons
an ocean never losing currents
a well in a desert that never runs out of water
a paint that never loses its colour amidst rain and the sun
a circle that goes on and on…
a love that comes once in a lifetime
that trumps all the love you have had in your life
and will have in the future

-the love i have for you

as the sun comes out in the morning, i think of you
and as it goes down in the evening, i think of you
as the moon claims its kingdom at night, i think of you
and as i close my eyes when i hit the hay, i think of you

why do i spend so much time writing about you? why do i spend so much time drafting you letters i will never send, that will just sit at the floor of my closet collecting dust, why? because it is not possible to use stardust as my ink and paint my love across the canvas of the universe for you, because it is not possible for all the world to hear me even if i shout about how much i love you from top of the Mount Fuji, but in this way, through writing, i could preserve you and my love for you, with my pen i could immortalize you in between the pages of a book. and after we both perish, my love for you will live on in these pages.

all i do every day all day is think of you
everywhere i go, you're there
every song i listen to, you're in it
every movie i watch, you're there as well
even in the air i breathe
every whisper from the rain
you're there, you're everywhere
even in my dreams
i could go to the darkest pit of the world
where darkness reigns
yet i'd still see you there brightly
you inhibit my whole existence
and i'm writing this because i'm so full of you

i cannot fathom trying to explain
how much you mean to me
you wouldn't understand
even i do not understand
so, the next best thing i can do is write about it

INK

your face, ingrained
your smile, ineffaceable
your gaze, haunting
your scent, lasting
your entire being
blazoning across the canvas of my heart indelibly

when my whole world is collapsing
and nothing feels right
knowing that you exist
knowing that you are out there somewhere
makes everything feel okay somehow

as vega and altair dance in the sky
as rigel sparks brightly
as a comet leaves a trail of dust behind
as andromeda whirls next to the milky way
my anorexic heart yearns for you

as the milky way waits to become one with andromeda
i wait for you my love
to recognize how much love this heart of mine holds for you
if you take my hand
i promise you will never have to fall again
i will hold you tight and never let go
twirl your fingers
lace it in mine
together, forever
we will be as irrevocable as milkdromeda will be

no force is strong enough
to calm the whirlpool of emotions
running in circles inside me
no hand is strong enough to hold me
and make me forget about you
no touch dear enough
to make me stop longing for your hands
which has never touched me
no gaze powerful enough
to make me stop dreaming about you
no love deep enough
to surmount the love i have for you

i cannot tell precisely what urges me to write this
maybe the faint hope that
if i get everything out on paper
my heart would not be too heavy
or maybe i am trying to transport you
here next to me through this letter
whatever it is, one thing is certain
i'm holding this pen for you
i'm writing on this paper for you
i'm thinking of you
it's always *you, you, you…*

i do not know
if i can still call my heart my own
when it is plunged in your blood
soaked in your soul
and drowned at the challenger deep
at the thought of you

your happiness is paramount to me
because my love
your smile is the single most beautiful art
i have ever seen
they are a mirror
to the cosmos soaring in the galaxy

i did not know it was possible
to love someone this much
every second of my life
every breath i take is dipped with your name
you are a drug i cannot get enough of

loving you
the most amazing
and selfless thing
i have ever done in my entire years of existence

the thing about you is that
i was not even searching when i found you
but when i did find you
you completed my heart in a way
it sheds light to my realization that
i have been living with half a heart until i found you

the sky knows how in love i am with you
six ways from sunday, my love

the love i have for you
is not something that can be whipped out
by forcing it inside a box
even then, the light inside the box
could still fulgurate everyone to blindness

the matter of the heart is irrational
it gives no heat to logical conclusions
and careful calculations of thoughts
and there is no reason to explain
why my wretched heart is so fixated on you
why i keep wanting you when i could have any other guy i want
other men could offer me the world
and yet, i would still choose to stay by your side in an underground dungeon
loving you until i'm nothing but hollow shells

there is a specific time for everything
a specific time is curved for everything
and you, oh you
you were made to be loved by me
through all eternity

you instil tranquillity
in my world of mayhem

have you ever just cried because you love someone too much? not because they
broke your heart or because you are sad. but because there is too much love for them
in your heart it gets heavy and weighs you down, and the only way to assuage the
heavy weight is to let moisture run down your cheeks.

sometimes when i gaze
upon your flawless being
your shimmering smile
your piercing doe eyes
i feel grateful to have eyes that can behold you
your existence makes this world a better place
if only, you could see yourself from my eyes my darling

-if only

even if you only end up my 'what if?'
i would forever treasure you
for you let me know how much love i have inside me
you make me feel emotions i never knew i had
make me feel love i never thought i was capable of feeling

-you, my darling, are my whole definition of love

i have burnt so long and so quiet inside, you must have wondered if i still love you, i do. look how long this love can stay without making a sound. look how quiet this love can be on the surface, when inside, it is filled with tornados and thunderous rumbling that can shake the very core of the earth, destroy life as we know it on earth. shatter all the rocks and mountains and drain all the water and crash with a massive sized asteroid and dissolve into tiny pieces of fragments and quietly float in nothingness until a black hole swallows everything inside and no fragments survive as they reach singularity. singularity defy our current understanding of physics, still, when those tiny pieces of the earth reach singularity, before they burn out and cease to exist, they would still scream your name, they would still burn out your name, they would shake the strong force of the black hole hallowing your name

look! look! how quiet this love can be

missing you comes in waves, like a storm, it took me and threw me around in the air, it tossed me around mercilessly from where i am through the darkest pit in the world, it brought all the chemicals in my brain to a halt, and wrapped me around in a blanket of your face and smell until i am so full of you that the only way i could breathe was to let the moisture in my eyes fall out as a means to express what my mouth can't pronounce.

why am i human? a mere human who could do nothing even when the simple thought of you brought me to tears. why am i not a sofa at your house? if i were a sofa at your house, i could be the one you rest on, i could be the one you approach when you're tired, and i could see you all day, i could just be there and look at you and that would be enough for me. tell me, why am i not a sofa at your house? if i had to travel through a four-dimensional world, searching for superior beings who could change the trajectory of our lives, i would find them even if it takes a thousand years, if only that would mean they could transform me to be a sofa at your house.

-i miss you, i'm sorry

Part Two

as the four walls of my room are my witness
they have heard, seen, and witness
the havoc you caused
the damage you have done
the rift you have created
to a heart that only has love for you

the total sum of my entire being
my heart
my blood
my soul
my life
they are yours to take
you can break them into different million pieces
cut them open and scatter the mess at your feet
for your own amusement
and yet, there would still be nothing i can do to stop you
cause they are not mine anymore

your name has been living in my heart for so long
when i asked to throw it out
it asks, "how can i throw away my owner?"

you have turned my innocent heart
which has not loved anyone before
to a sanguinary field

-bleeding for you

one look at you
and it petrifies me
oh God, it petrifies me
of what i would do for you
anything, anything
my bleeding heart is on the ground for you

i cannot count the times
i have stayed up late at night
yearning for you
craving you
crying for you
you have robbed so many sleeps from me

how come i feel you
so near in my heart
when in reality
you are so far away from me?

letting go is the greatest act of love. when you love someone, you want to spend every waking moment with them, you want to be as close to them as possible, but when you realize, they may be better off without you, they may be happier without you, it is a hard pill to swallow. if you love yourself more and value your happiness above theirs, you would not give a hoot about letting them go, you would pursue them to the point of exhaustion until they say yes out of misery, there, you achieved your goal, your desire, your happiness. but what of theirs? the willingness to let go is the most selfless, most pure, form of love there could ever be. and because i love you more than i love myself, i let you go. i let you go when all i wanted was to hold on to you, i let you go when i cried myself to sleep every night missing you, i let you go when the first thing i do in the morning is cry because i saw you in my dreams and i so wanted that dream to be my reality, i let you go when all i wanted was to be in your embrace, i let you go when it was the hardest thing to do, i let you go because i wanted you to be happy. and if your happiness is not with me, i want you to go where it is. do not feel bad for me, my love for you is so great that it trumps all the heartbreak you have caused, you can have all the girls and mistresses you want, you can trample upon my heart and tear it into pieces and spit on it, it still would not be enough to make me hate you, nothing can make me hate you, go and be happy. that is all i want. for you to be happy.

-i let you go because i love you more than i love me.

maybe in another life
maybe in another universe
i would not let you go
i will hold you tight
i will not let you let me go
i will stay at your feet
begging you to see my love
maybe...maybe...

i love you too much
i wonder if it is even right
to love another this much

there's nothing i would not do for you
even walking away from you
even if that is the last thing i want to do

my heart is bleeding
and it reeks of you and you alone

there are some days
when the pain of longing for you
the pain of missing you
the pain of craving you
the pain of loving you
is bearable
sometimes i can breathe fine
sometimes i can sleep
but there are sometimes
the pain just punches in the lungs
blocks my windpipe
and leave me grasping for air

your silence is deafening
to ears that only want to hear your voice

to love, is to suffer
to love, is to sacrifice
to love, is to surrender
to love, is to endure
to love, is to embrace
to love, is to tolerate
there can be no love otherwise

the only succour i have
is my pen and paper
and here i am
writing about it
cause that's the only thing i can do
to soothe my hurting heart
a heart that only wanted a chance to love you
a heart that never got the chance to

i may love you
until the day my heart stops beating
but i will burn my hand
in Dante's seventh circle of hell
before i ever reach out to you again

missing you
is the most vicious
atrocious
and bestial battle
i have to grapple every waking day

the pen in my hand
the notebook on my table
the only consolation i have

when i miss you a little too much
writing about it is the only way
i can express how much i miss you
when i have no right to

– but i do

swimming in the ocean of tears
i shed for you
help, my love
i'm drowning in this wave of love

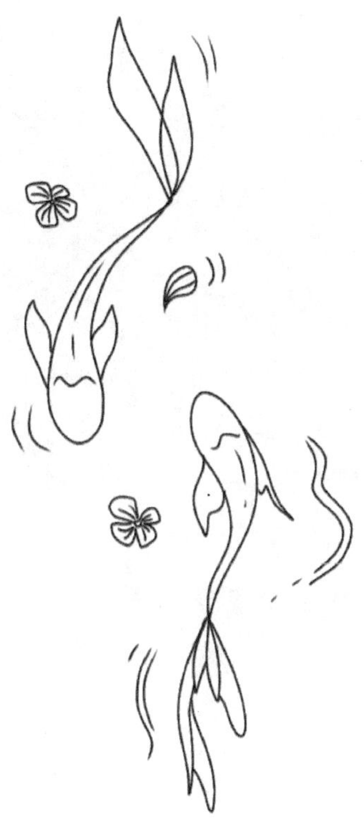

Part Three

i love you
i have to deal with it

now that i know this kind of love exists
now that i feel what i feel
now that i know what i know
how can i ever settle for less?
in other words
how can i ever settle for someone else that's not you?

if one day
you decided to come to me
i'd say, "welcome home, i've been waiting for you"

seconds, minutes
days, months, years
have passed by
i still love you as much as i did on the day you left
if not more
what does that say of my love?
if it is not true

you have made such a home
inside my heart
that some feral part of you will always inhibit
no matter how far apart we are
or how long we haven't talked

Somewhere in an alternate universe

our bodies crooked and bent
our skins sagged
our eyesight blurry
our children running around
mirth overflowing from them
we watch the sunset for the thousandth time
we always do
because you love sunsets
the sun begins to retreat for the day
you ask if i love the sunset
my darling, i love you
so much so that i love everything you love
in addition to loving you
i love the sunsets because it reminds me of you
i love the moon because it reminds me of your eyes
i love the sun because it parallels your smile
and God, i love this world, because you are in it
i love you. till the end of time

-always

you think i haven't tried? you think i enjoy rotting away pining for you? you think i haven't tried to move on? oh, i've tried, the stars know i've tried, i've tried, i've tried, for so long. but this stupid obsessive heart of mine does not listen to me anymore, from the day it starts beating for you, i lose all control over them. until and unless you give it back, i will pine for you, i will keep on craving you, i will continue rotting away for you, and you know the irony is? even you do not have the power to give me back my heart. it can sit at your door without you battling an eyelid to it, it can sit at your door when it's freezing outside without you giving a damn, and yet it will stay.

i do not know
if i will ever be able to love anyone
the way i loved you
that's what makes you so special
i may love someone new someday
but you'd always be *my first great love*

there is a part of me
that will always love you
a part that is yours
a part no one can take over
a part that is
and will be forever reserved by you

you were an unexpected collision
a thunderous bolt
that twist and turn my heart
culminating into near madness

what if i don't stop loving you?
what if i keep on loving you and bleed my heart away?
what if i forget myself trying to hold on to your memories?
what if even after a thousand years, my telling i love you does not mean a thing?
what if loving you is my curse?
one i cannot stop
one i can never have either
and i must live half alive
because of it

i search for you
in everyone i meet

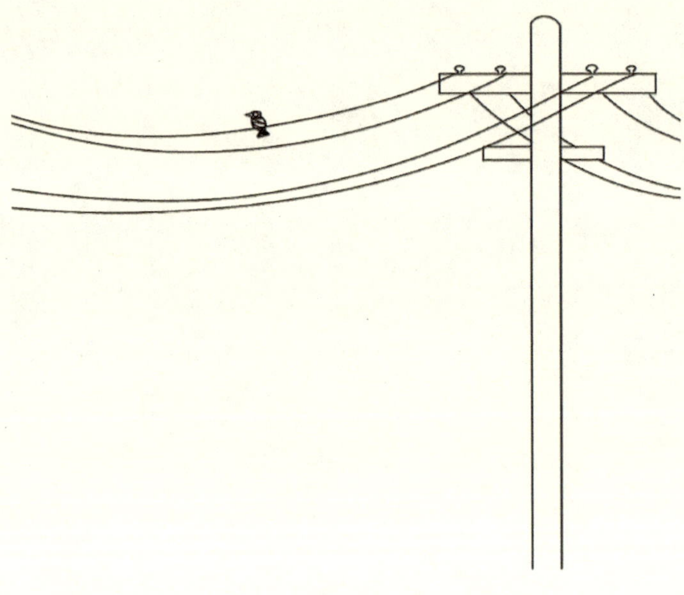

why do i hate other men?
because darling
they are a realization that
i cannot love anyone like you
they make me realize that
there is no place left in my heart for anyone else

when i lay under six feet ground
when i lay motionless inside the earth
where no worries and troubles can reach me
when all trepidation is stuck in yesterday
when there is no tomorrow
i would be glad i got to meet you in my lifetime
i would be glad i got to love you

fifty years later, i will look back and read the letters i wrote you and remember how in love i used to be with you. i would shake my head thinking how stupid my younger self had been, to think she would ever get over and stop loving you. because fifty years later, i would still love you just as much as i did on october 2023.

on my deathbed
if they ask me
what love is
i would say your name

i have become yours
without you ever touching me

if loving you is wrong
i do not ever want to be right

oh moon, i ask you
will you protect my love for me?
make sure no ill will befallen him
in the darkest of night
oh sun, i ask you
will you protect my love for me?
make sure he is happy
do not let the smile on his face go away
please, please

in this world where people say
true love does not exist
i can smile and shake my head
because i know it exists
how else would i explain what i feel for you?
i know true love exists, because of my love for you

-i am proof that true love exists

i used to think
awards and achievements
recognition and success
are what matters
now i know better
all the awards and success in this world
would not matter
if i don't have you
and if i have you
even if i don't have any recognition and fame
i'd still be the richest and happiest woman on earth

-my happiness lies with you

if a deadly virus gets out
and you turn into a zombie
i'd let you bite me
i'd rather be a zombie with you
than remain a human without you

never was i a patient person
sometimes a 3-minute song is too long
sometimes i cut movies when i'm only 10 minutes in
but you
oh, for you, i have all the patience in the world
i'd wait for you even if you're a hundred years late

-for you, anything

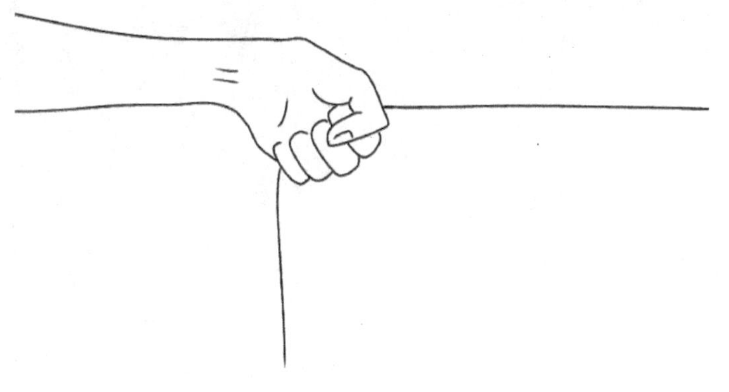

as each petal fell
my heart beats for you
as each branch withers
my heart beats for you
as each pond vacates
my heart beats for you
as each day passes
my heart beats for you
it stops knowing how to beat for anyone but you

i would gather stardust
and moonbeam
trying to write a rhapsody for you
lingering on canvas
using space sparkles to capture your face
pressing on black and white keys
aiming to produce tunes
that parallels the rhythm of your heartbeat

as your eyes smiled at me
i knew
knew
deep in my bones
that's the sight i want to see every day
for the rest of my life

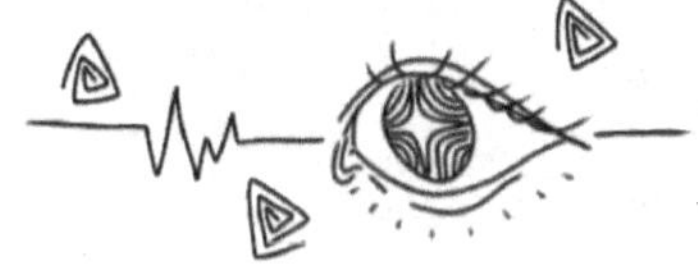

i am but a meat-covered skeleton
an old soul
trapped in a feeble fragile girl's body
but heavens help me
i would grab the ankle of thunder itself
hammering it with my pleading
trapped the stars so that the sky is blank
make a bargain with the sun to leave earth in utter darkness
until chaos and havoc reign upon mankind
than to see you hurt
i would return to dust
and boil into oblivion
than to see you hurt
i would surrender to be a prey
for the denizens of the forest
to fill up their belly
than to see you hurt
i would tear the skin off of anyone
dislocate their bones
and throw them in the river
to be feasted upon
by creatures dwelling underground
to anyone trying to hurt you

am i stupid enough
to wait for you
after all these times?
when it is not certain
you are even coming back?

-i have lost all sense of rationality when it comes to you

DECEMBER
31

i dream of you
even when i'm awake
i dream of you
when my eyes are open
i dream of you
when i'm in the presence of others
i dream of you
in between the breeze that past when i blink

-how weird to dream of someone
when i'm not even sleeping

if i'd get an option
to never experience an ounce of hurt
by never falling in love with you
in the first place
i'd still choose to experience all the heartbreaks
because no matter how bad it was
loving you was the most amazing thing that happened to me
it's strong enough to cover all the scars
in my heart

-no, the hurt didn't outweigh the love

i've never liked my name so much
but when it comes out of your mouth
it becomes the most beautiful symphony
a girl could ever wish to hear

"you cannot love others,
until you love yourself first"
it's a complete utter bullshit
i have never loved myself the way i love you
i have never loved anyone the way i love you
you taught me how a person
can love one another
in ways i didn't know was possible
you made me aware of how much love
i have inside myself
because of you
i've learnt to love myself
you have ignited
the lover girl in me
the hopeless romantic in me
and because i love you
i've learnt to love other things too

-this is why i call you not by your name,
but call you 'love'

i've always had the flair for dramatics
but to be haunted
by someone who's not even dead
is a bit over the line

-will you ever stop haunting me?

as much as i love life
there is no forever
as much as i wish to go to mars
everything is temporary
as much as i want to succeed in life
nothing lasts forever
in this world of uncertainty
where everything is constantly changing
and the only thing permanent is
how temporary everything is
i do not mind being temporary with you
as long as i get to hold your hand
i will be temporary with you

how can you ever die?
if you live between these pages

i'm grateful for you
for you give me the chance
to experience the fairy tale love in my life
the kind of love we read in books
the kind of love we see in the movies
the kind of love being sung in songs

i do not have to tell people about you
they have seen you
sparkling in my eyes
in the bubbles of my laugh
in the lingering smell of me
in between every word enunciated from my mouth

in this contemporary world of digital influence and societal pressures hovering above our heads, where the new generations of people have forgotten the art of love, the importance of giving effort, the significance of falling in love and finding true love. where most people think true love doesn't even exists. when a person is elated when their partner does the barest minimum of texting back, when flowers are not delivered to people's doorsteps anymore, when letters are not hand-written for people anymore, when 'yo, you got snap?' is the line people used to express the once of interest they have in people now. i am glad i got to meet you, i am glad i got to meet the one boy whom i love enough to write a whole book about, the one boy whom i would fight for until the end of time, the one boy i would give all my efforts for, the one boy who has taught me the art of love.

because of you, this world is a thousand-fold more beautiful, love

i met you when i was nineteen
i'm well aware
of the nineteenth love theory
but i'm glad it's you
i met when i was nineteen
if someone is going to be
my greatest tragedy
it means
it's also the greatest love of my life
i wouldn't want anyone else
but you to be
my greatest love
my greatest tragedy

you are the line between everything i write
the sigh between every breath i take
the sight the corner of my eye searches everywhere
the tune the keys of my heart
has been trying to find

don't you love him a little too much?
they asked
too much
is my middle name
i answered

if i have one lucky star
i'd wish for you
if i have hundred lucky stars
i'd wish a hundred times for you

Acknowledgements

I believe in giving credits where credits are due, but right now, I'm only going to give credits where it's really due. And unlike my other books' acknowledgements, where I used up pages and pages, this one will be short.

First, a sincere thanks and my utmost gratitude go to my saviour and Lord, Jesus Christ. Nothing would be possible without Him.

Second, I'd like to thank my parents, for treating me like a precious rare gem since the day I was born, but most of all, for their unwavering support of my writing career.

Third, to my brother, Gideon, for having the most embarrassing childhood stories of our sibling, but most of all, for always being one phone call away when I need you, even though you're a thousand miles away from home.

Fourth, to my high lady, Dinsangi, for loving all the fictional characters I love as much I do, for always reading the books I recommended to you that I say will destroy you emotionally, but most of all, for being the best supporter a writer friend could ask for, for always making sure I have my head in the right direction, and for always believing in me.

Last but not least, to Francis_16, for making all the heart-rending illustrations for this book. Your help and assistance were invaluable to me.

www.ingramcontent.com/pod-product-compliance
Lightning Source LLC
La Vergne TN
LVHW090940150826
845672LV00006B/1565

* 9 7 9 8 8 9 7 2 4 1 0 0 2 *